FOR-GIVING
GROUND

FOR-GIVING GROUND

Poems for Living and Praying

by

Irene Zimmerman, OSF

FRANCISCAN HERALD PRESS
1434 West 51st Street ● Chicago, Illinois 60609

Library of Congress Cataloging in Publishing Data

Zimmerman, Irene.
    For-Giving ground.

    I. Title. II. Title: For-Giving ground.
PS3576.I5115F6   1986   811'.54   86-25687
ISBN 0-8199-0903-3

I finally saw my life: a mystery of
a wandering sheep forever loved and found,
and rather than that lilac paradise,
chose instead this firm for-giving ground.

(Homecoming)

To all those who taught me
that life is for-giving:

my friends,
family
and the School Sisters of St. Francis

CONTENTS

Part 1. GROWING

Part 2. LETTING GO

Part 3. TRUSTING

Part 1
GROWING

I stumble
through
my past
to future
tense
somehow

in restless
search
for You
who are
the present
perfect
NOW.

(In Tense)

TO BE OR NOT TO BE BUTTERFLY

To leave this cocoon
on these fragile wings?

To dare a new world
and the risk it brings?

To answer a Voice
that persistently sings?

3

DESERT DAY

I went to the desert one morning
with Exodus, chapter three,
and walked with Moses through the sand
to where the bush was burning.
I was not surprised
it did not turn to ash,
for so it had been burning
since my childhood days.

But suddenly I heard
a voice call out to me
from that bush:
"Pay attention."

Moses left.
"Take off your shoes," God said,
"for the life on which you stand
is holy.
Feel it beneath your feet,
supporting you.
I am THE ONE WHO IS
and this is how I hold you."

I stood barefoot on the ground
of my life history,
burning through and through
with that mystery.

SEARCH

I rummage through
my childhood years—
old dresser drawers
that wait for me
to pick their locks
and find my hidden self.

RESPONSE

"It's only some fungi," she said,
with condescending nod of head
to my ninety-ninth question
on the day I discovered the world.

Little myself,
I loved those petals of parasite
and kept them, despite her disdain,
on my shelf.

DISCOVERY

I ran to the house excitedly:
"Come and see
the most beautiful thing in the world!"
She could not refuse the ecstatic news
of the three-year-old tugging girl
and came out to where a necklace of pearl
and gold and orange rings
was sunning itself on the lawn near the swings.

Then suddenly, shocked, disbelieving,
sure it was all a mistake,
I watched as she ran for an ax
and killed that jewel of a snake.

DAISIES

When we reached the peak
overlooking the lake,
mother, whose sonoric symphony
had entertained us through
the last half hour of miles,
snored to a sudden finale and said,
"Ach, wie schön!
Let's stop and look at the daisies."

All the way up,
other flowers had tried,
with pink and lavender wiles,
to charm her. But she,
ensconced in the back of the Olds,
her straw hat askew to block the sun,
had passed them by
with soporific indifference.

We all piled out to inhale
the Upper Michigan air
and to bring her a few
of the simple flowers.
She buried her nose in them,
then lifted a pollen-powdered face
to smile at us
with sunny daisy grace.

I haven't traveled that road again,
but wherever daisies grow,
mother shines in my inner sky
and I warm in that afterglow.

AN OLD-FASHIONED GIRL

My mother was old-fashioned, she
refused to buy the tyranny
of style.
Hemlines rose or fell each year—without her.
So too,
she stayed short despite the spike-heeled shoe.
Other women, when the coiffeurs plotted,
let their hair be snipped or curled accordingly.
My mother kept her dignity
and head,
serenely knotted.
The whittled waistline came and went—
she stayed steadfast, ample.
Nor was time spent
debating color combinations—whether
green and blue could go together, for example.
"Ach Gott," she'd say with impish smile,
"He painted sky and trees that way—
I guess He too is out of style."

I doubt she'd even *heard* of Mrs. Jones,
but she wore an ancient wisdom in her bones.

BLINDNESS
(for Frau Grabe)

"Come," (poor blind friend) I said,
"let me show you the river.
The ducks look so proud:
'See how clever
my little ones are,' they strut.
The swans are hard put
to outdo them.
There's not a cloud
in the sky. Feel the sun
on your face?"

I chattered on and on
till with quiet grace
she smiled at me
and I learned how to see.

EXCHANGE

"Yes," said Mary,
filled with grace.
"Yes," said the Word,
and took on a human face.

CHRISTMAS SKY

That once-in-a-world-time night
even the stars, otherwise
so distant in their ancient skies,
came to adore the in-the-beginning Light.

Jew-EL

As Simeon walked
with wisdom and age
down the temple corridor,
his eyes,
searching through candlelight,
dimly told him of a woman
waiting,
her body wrapped around
her infant son
with reverent joy.

He bent toward the small Jew
(the small jewel
set in a brooch of mothering arms)
and his beard, touching,
tingled alive as telegraph wires
telling the good news:
      "What
        hath
        God
        wrought!"

Old eyes saw
an infinite Light,
old hands
cradled the face,
grace poured.
No one spoke
till "Now,"
his old voice broke,
"You may dismiss Your servant,
Lord."

Irene Zimmerman

AMARYLLIS

You arrived a week ago,
pushing at the lid
of the box where you hid.
Tonight—New Year's Eve—
you stand tiptoe,
trying, I believe,
to catch time at its turning
and give it a swing
straight into spring.

Patience, amaryllis!
We have little power
to change time's pace,
but we do have this hour
to bring into bloom
our own inner space.

AWAKENING

I took an early morning winter walk
and stopped to rest beneath a snow-filled tree.
Everything was very still until
it woke and shook its bedding out on me.

SPRING HATCHING

New grass,
incubated
to full term by sun, cracks
open the hard shell of winter's
last snow.

HERO

"Do not disturb!"
the sign reads.

Behind the wire
of the turkey pen
stands brave Tom
with tail spread
and eyes of fire
protecting his hen
from a field of weeds.

Irene Zimmerman

LATE SPRING SEASON: REASON

Bat-and-balled,
overalled,
out spring crept.
Wagon hauled,
puppy called,
puddle lept.
Icy—slipped.
Caterwauled,
homecrawled,
muddy—whipped.
Wept.
Slept.
(Can't come out again, they say,
till middle of May.)

MATINEE

Ten swallows sit
on a telephone wire
and stridently twit.
From a post opposite,
one bird—to whit,
the primadonna of the choir,
directs (she's a liar
if she doesn't admit
it's quite the reversal
of an orderly) rehearsal.

NEW-HATCHED TURKEY

Wobbling on stilts
that threaten
to collapse
against your cardboard
walls, taking two
seconds (or
was it three
this time)
of shut-eye before
you open those bright
black buttons and try
once more,

you haven't
done a thing
to deserve it,
but here are four
adults, each
with a master's degree
and other loads
of importance,
holding their breath
and wondering if
you'll make that next
step.

You could teach
the networks
how to up their ratings,
but they'd only say,
"You turkey!" if I
were to tell them that,
so they can just
keep talking upstairs
with their stilted scripts
while here in the basement,
we stay glued
to your every
move.

VIOLET

Had I been here an hour ago,
I might have seen you thrust
your tiny tendrils through the just
unfrozen earth.

What urgent longing
lets you risk so much
to brave the touch
of what-you-do-not-know,
tear the weave
of last year's growth and leave
your dark security to greet
whatever lives above you?

Violet, I love you!
Fragile though you seem,
you give me courage
as I go to meet
the day that calls me forth
beyond the dream.

BLOODROOT

I found you on Good Friday's dawn
blooming white! white!
eight woven petals lifted up
to hold sunlight.

I didn't know what to call you
and, when I knelt to cup
your brightness, thought of "Easter flower."
You seemed a splendid sign—
perhaps I could bypass the Cross and find
the Risen Christ already waiting
in the garden of this early morning hour.

Then someone came
and let me know your name:
Bloodroot! I wondered who
had found the red sap at your center
and, feeling wise for seeing through
your lovely outside show,
named you so.

The name I gave is just as true:
your centered suffering is transformed in sun.
In you blood grows to Easter—
blooms to ONE.

CENTERING

I walk
  my restless breathing
   in and out until
    it's quieted

sit

watch
  the flame
   curl round the wood
  the smoke
   try to smother it
  a spark
   wing the log
    with crack and spit

see
  the wood
   consent to fire,
   expire
    in a blaze of

ecstasy.

SMALL TALK BY A SEASHELL

You made me small.
Sometimes a grain
of sand slips in;
I can't see out!
For days that's all
I think about.
Sometimes the wall
is paper-thin,
and I see clearly,
out and in.

You made me
small.
Help me be
and love it all.

DUET

Today I heard Your voice,
deep bass violed,
and piccoloed around You
like a happy child.

HELP ME BE GENTLE, GENTLE GOD

Help me be gentle, gentle God:
as I wade along this shore,
let me not disdain one grain of sand,
nor take one careless step and by it break
the tiny, fragile petal of a shell
meant someday perhaps to house a pearl.

A MAZE OF GRACE

God burst the bonds of boundlessness
and built a world so timed and placed
that now our search for All-at-Once
draws us through a where-and-when
until we learn our loneliness
and pray to be found back again.

CENTERING MOMENTS

I

On such a dawn—
a sudden blaze of trees!
I take my shoes off,
fall upon my knees.

II

I walk through woods
at slow procession pace
and find You, gentle God,
in Queen Anne's lace.

III

God, there's not much time—
I must be brief—
just now Your sun was smiling
on a leaf.

IV

I've wandered, lonely,
through long desert days.
Now tonight You've set
the stars ablaze.

ECSTASY'S END

I wanted to stay
on the Tabor and shout
"Praise God" all day.
But You went away
and the light went out.

IN TENSE

I stumble
through
my past
to future
tense
somehow

in restless
search
for You
who are
the present
perfect
NOW.

Part 2
LETTING GO

I receive my life again,
returning from not-knowing,
and try not to snatch it up
and bury it somewhere
for safekeeping,
try to lay
it in God's hands all night.
The wind keeps blowing.

(All Night the Wind)

TOWARD INTEGRATION

Learning to unsay
the childhood messages that play
on sterile strings,
to be a note that soars and sings,
attuned to human touch and sighs . . .
learning, God, to praise with human cries.

ANNIVERSARY PRAYER

Mother, made whole today
of all your brokenness,
remember the cracked clay
your daughter still is.

O GOD, IF BY SOME MIRACLE

O God, if by
some miracle
You can unmake
this hardened clay
I pray You, take
me in Your hands
again and give

me suppleness
of tree that I
may bow and live.

TREE-TISE

I saw
a tree
today
that wasn't
going
anywhere—
had simply
stopped
growing.
It wasn't
high
enough
to let
me think
maybe
it tried
to reach
the sky
and died,
trying.
No branch.
No leaf.
Thin.
Straight.
A sad
attempt
at being
a tree,
exempt
from love
and hate.

I'd rather send some branches out
to hug the world,
be blown around a bit
even if I ended up lopsided.
I'd rather show
some blights and scars than grow
so damn
u
p
r
i
g
h
t
e
d.

STORM AND AFTERMATH

I

O how good it feels
to pitch in and help You, Jesus,
throw the money-changing tables to the floor
and watch the pigeons fly in frantic freedom,
circle overhead, descend again to sit, unsure,
on their broken cage's swinging door.

O how good to vent my rage—
to overturn the full, fat jars
and see the thin
coins spill, crazily spin—
released from the abuse made of them
to buy and sell Your praise.

II

It is evening now.
The storm is past; the temple floor
swept clean.
Here on the hillside where You weep
for the sinful city in them and me
that makes Your love a thing
of trade, I come to lay
my money-changer heart before You;
creep
beneath Your warm, forgiving wing.

NIGHT THOUGHTS

I took a solitary walk tonight
and found someone had locked the moon
behind the branches of a stalwart oak.
She looked at me with open face,
and though she spoke
no word, I knew
her innocence. What to do?
I simply walked a little farther east
and thus released
her. Oh, if only I could free
the ones I've thrown to prison in my mind
so easily—
dissolve all bars,
walk with them in peace beneath the stars!

THESE GRAINS OF SAND

Lodged between my shoe and toe
so self-inflated,
persistent as my sins
and like them, hated—
help me someday understand,
Jesus, please,
that You make pearls to grow
from such as these.

HUNGER

I'm starved for your homey bread and wine
and the honey of your smile across the room.
Since you've gone
everything I touch is only stone.

LETTER

Penpoints of light
erasing the night.

ABSENCE

I wander through
the empty,
aching
caves
carved
by the river
of my longing
for you
and listen to
echoes of
your visits.

TO MY HUSBAND DYING
(for Mrs. Arnold Rettig)

I didn't think your death would come so soon—
that its pitiless high noon would blaze
between the quiet covers of this night.
I've watched you now for hours, past all sleep,
energized by thirty years together,
and tried to let you go beyond my kisses
pressed upon your poor distorted face.
I would not keep you back, comatose,
when light is bending round the ending tunnel,
but dear, I've had no time to say goodby.
My body, left still warm by your embrace,
cannot let you go without a cry!

STEWARDSHIP

I went out to gather wood,
threw it piece by piece beside the stove,
and planned—when it got cold enough—
to build a fire.

It was so thoughtlessly simple,
so seemingly good.
Then I became aware
of trembling wood.

DEFENSE BUILD-UP

We are small children
in a pile of crackling leaves
playing with matches.

FALL AND SPRING

After the soldiers had disappeared
and the chopper had flown away
with the body of the unseasoned boy,
a woman stared at the field
and grieved for the mangled grain.
It little mattered to her anymore
whose body had spilled across her crops:
she had seen too much of war.
And as for freedom, what good
was that when the grain was gone?

A Kansas woman later
turned away from growing fields
to grieve at new grass on the grave
of the too soon harvested boy.
What good that the grain should grow
when the son was gone?

WORD GATHERING

All afternoon I gathered words.
Now I place them carefully,
phrase by phrase,
with space enough for breathing.

Dead words!
God, make them blaze
as we gather in this fearful
night of days.

CHRISTMAS PRAYER FOR A NUCLEAR AGE

Christ, we've lost the entrance to Your cave,
killed the stars with our neon lights,
amplified our discords till we've drowned
the sound of angels' song and silent nights.

We've made our Earth into a burial ground:
conceiving MX silos in her womb,
constructing monuments of missile towers,
and planting radar flowers on the tomb.

We fear the almost midnight of these hours,
know we could be aborted on the way,
yet dare to hope, on this brink of grave,
that You will save us with a Christmas Day.

MINISTRY OF THE POOR

Unless you love me,
do not give me food.
I have no strength against
your white, pagan bread—
it ferments in me
like starvation working
in the swollen-bellied children
of black Africa.

Give me instead one whole kernel
of yourself.
Put it carefully into my hand
and look at me.
That will hold me
for this day.
(As for tomorrow,
I am in God's hands.)

WAITING

In the intimate, candlelit
church I waited, longing for You, God,
to hold me in Your mothering embrace.
You did not come. I left without a prayer.

Later You looked hungrily at me
from my lonely brother's broken face.
In that awful moment full of grace
I learned that You are waiting everywhere.

ALL NIGHT THE WIND

All night
the wind keeps blowing
at my window.
The almost winter
is here again.
"Where did the year go?"
we ask each other
in puzzled surprise, and
hiding behind that mask, ask,
"Where do the years go? where
does time go?
where am I
going?"
All night
the wind keeps blowing.
The doctor called yesterday
to say, "No malignancy."
I receive my life again,
returning from not-knowing,
and try not to snatch it up
and bury it somewhere
for safekeeping,
try to lay
it in God's hands all night.
The wind keeps blowing.

DISCIPLESHIP

Resolute,
You turn Your face
toward Jerusalem,
tell us You must go
and why You must.

Fearfully,
with slow slow pace,
I follow
dry as dust.

CREATION II

In the desert Jesus found the shards—
broken idols
staring from empty sockets.

Bullets of sun shot him in the eyes.
Wild beasts leaped,
their hot breath scorching his face.

He fought off the mirages.

Ahead was a cool running stream
where He could lie down.

Over Him bent the Potter.

> "Father, I didn't know
> to be human would be so hard.
> In the beginning before the world,
> it was easy to say *yes*—
> to believe I could love them all
> even unto death!"

"My Child! My Firstborn!
I will not *make* you be
this time.
If you so choose, you may stay
along this river bank—
my beautiful sculptured clay
shaped like a human one.

"I, your Potter, will love you.

"I will try to forget
the undone children of my womb.
They are a grief to me anyway."

Jesus remembered the shards
with their soulless eyes.
Should he be one of them?

The Potter waited . . .
holding Their breath!

FAREWELL AT BETHANY: MARTHA
(Luke 10: 38-42)

I was caught in a dizzying chase
like an overwrought bee
buzzing from flower to flower
and hauling a honey harvest
home to an isolate tree.

Thanks for halting my absurd pace
and Mary-ing me.

FAREWELL AT BETHANY: MARY
(Lk 10: 38-42)

"Jesus, what a child I am—
 I didn't even think
 to offer You a drink!"

"Child, full of grace,
 I drank my fill
 from your listening face."

ENTRY
(Jn 12: 12-17)

Like a king He came,
astride a steed adorned with regal cloak,
to receive the crowd's acclaim:
"Hosanna! Blessed be the Name
of the Lord!" It was a gentle joke—
His prancing horse a borrowed colt,
jittery in the crowd, ready to bolt
back home with all its purple rags.

Before He turned their messianic hope
completely upside down,
He rode to Calvary majestically—
a clown.

SOME WOMEN STOOD BENEATH THE CROSS
(Mt 27: 55-56)

Their friend was hanging on the Cross!
They were at a total loss
for ways to help him—clearly knew
that there was nothing they could do.
Obscene hecklers leered at them.
Passers-by jeered at them:
"Some King you've got up there—some clown!"
They could not, would not let him down.

The women simply, strongly stood
loving him beneath the wood.

"DARKNESS CAME OVER THE WHOLE LAND"
(Lk 23:45)

Last night the sky was falling!
I ran inside to hide—
locked the door,
drew the blind,
and cowered in a corner of my mind
until I heard You calling
and partly understood the reason for
Good Friday:
unless You break our sky apart
and let us stand in rain,
we cannot see You on the other side
of pain.

JOURNEY WITH THE SHADOW

"Your poems are beautiful,
but ponderous," you said,
and bade me run the Umbrian hills
sandal-light as Francis.

I try but, friend,
my life still shadows me
and I must struggle not to send
that wild child into night again.

This far at least I've come: yesterday
I found the Abraham-trail, gathered wood,
and grieving, headed for the hidden hill,
the child on my shoulder.

Oh, how I love it, fear it!—
fear its sweet hot breath
will steal my heart and I may final-choose
to be like god, refuse that death.

Pray that I may make the offering,
receive my life new-gifted from the Lamb.
O then I'll run, sandal-free as Francis,
wring my song like sunshine on the hills.

CONVERSION

In my childhood days I read the words,
"Keep pure. Remain unsullied from the world,"
and thought this meant to stay good-little-girled.
When I heard You say, "Follow me,"
I followed You, of course. But afterwards
I found those awful people in Your crowd
and picked my way quite gingerly, afraid
I would be judged to be naive, or worse—
"one of them." I was, I must confess,
revolted too by all that sinfulness.

Soon I grew adept at playing games—
sometimes calling sin some nicer names,
sometimes bravely standing with the crowd
that stoned the people for their sex or drugs
or drink (though feeling some disquiet as of
late: if all my people hadn't been
so safe and soundly good, I'm not so sure
I would have stayed so innocent and pure).

Today I watch You as You reach the Hill.
You've carried all their burdens on Your back
and now You stretch Your body on that rack
to save Your alcoholics, prostitutes
and all who follow You to ask for healing.
And me? Mine is such a little sin,
so *venial* it's even hard to find
a name for it—a slavish search to please,
an awkwardness that holds me back from giving,
a fearful, shy retreat from deeply living.

I panic even now, afraid to be
alone with You at last, afraid to say
I am a sinner too. Christ, help me grow
to be a self where Life can freely flow.

PARABLE OF THE SEED

God
does it all, I know—
gives the sun, soil, rain

and yet . . . and yet!
(sweat your blood, my soul,
crushed in pain,
crying)

I
must let the seed grow,
must let
go,
must do the dying.

PASCHAL HOUR
(Jn 20)

You hurricaned me
to the base of a tree
at the crest of a hill
and watched me spill
my untold torrents
of fears.

Choking from words
honed long ago
on my flesh and bone—
"Don't touch me!"—
and gasping to give
who I thought I should be
to that god of stone,
but longing to live,
I paged to John
and suddenly heard
not *"Don't touch"*
but *"Don't cling,"*
and squeezed through the opening
of that narrow word!

There were still walls and walls.
I was still caught inside.
Then You came to me
(passing through easily)
with that wound torn wide,
exposing Your heart:
"You want to be woman?
Touch me and start."

JOURNEY'S END

I'm afraid to follow You.
I know how the story ends—
"No greater love than this:
    to lay down one's life
    for one's friends."

JUST NOW IT WAS RAINING

Just now it was raining,
though the sun was shining
(or though the sun was shining
it was raining).
The world could not decide its mood
nor wait—with so much life to live—
to give in organized, sedate
fashion: all-uncued,
it spilled a whole sunshine-shower
in half an hour.

So Spirit, spill Your rainy sun on me,
tangled up in ambiguity.

GOD OF SHELTER, GOD OF RAIN
(Is 4:6)

God of shelter
from the rain,
God of shade
from the heat,
I run from You
through the muddy street
of my uncommitted heart
and from the pain
of desert days

till wild winds beat
against my doors,
blasting sand
through all my walls,
and I stand
undone,
without retreat,

feel Your breath
in my ears,
Your command
to be the wheat,
to submit
to winnowing.

Sweet the giving.
Sweet this land.

God of shelter.
God of rain.
God of shade.
God of heat.

HALFWAY HOME

halfway home now
halfway into loving living
halfway into being-one-with
long past midnight
moving toward dawn

too late (thank God!)
to say I am
pure spirit
I am not incarnate
I will not serve You
with tenderness and affection
but only with intelligence
and good honest hard work by God!

halfway into saying truly
You have formed my inmost being
You knit me in my mother's womb
I give You thanks
that I am fearfully
wonderfully made
wonderful
are Your works!

halfway into receiving
two broken halves
of me from Your hands
and humbly helping You
to put them together
with reverence

halfway whole

Thank God.

VIGIL

Somewhere in the dark
between the Alpha
and Omega
You call me
out beyond myself.

Stumbling,
I strain to follow,
wanting to be, O
God-caught-up
and carried.

But lo!
Who is this lying
in the shadowed garden,
this human shivering Plea,
this caught-between-the-Agony-
and-Dying,

this (dear God no!)
crushed Christ crying!

WAIT FOR ME, JESUS

Wait for me, Jesus,
on Your way to the Tree.
Don't move out of sight.

Up, I know,
is the only way to grow,
but I'm so loaded down with me

and it is night.

Irene Zimmerman

CALVARY

Seared by the pain
of knowing
my sin,

sickened by the din
of the frenzied
crowd,

I huddle
near Your mother
in the pouring

red

rain.

STORM

A worn sun calls, "All is well."
Now in darkness, rising seas
of raging wind conspire to fell
the masts of ash and maple trees.

Irene Zimmerman

LISTEN TO THE FALL

Listen to the fall, O listen,
listen to the fall!
Trees fill the sky
with resonating, resignating sigh;
their leaves—a mottled mass of tangled,
tattered tangerine—cry
a solemn, slow, sustained good-by:
"It is finished." All
life converges in one final breath
of praise to You, my God, for Sister Death.

IN THE NIGHT THE SNOW

In the night the snow came eagerly—
gave itself to every house and tree,
filling every crevice, every crack,
and holding absolutely nothing back.

Help me, God, let go
wholeheartedly as snow.

ON PRAYING

Why
do you try
to tell me how
to be your God?
It is I
who have loved you
into Now.

When you pray,
simply say
"Our Father! Our Mother!"
till that day
you learn from me
the ONE WHOLE WORD.

Let me be
in you
the I AM I am.

PROCESS

Yes to falling and to rotting.
Yes to growing and to grinding.
Yes to kneading and to baking.
Yes to being bread, breadmaking God.

Part 3
TRUSTING

but
those
who
give
their
all
in
trust

are
raised
from
dust.

(Paradox)

PARADOX

The one who clings like last year's leaves
afraid to fall to waiting field,
and never learns to yield,
forever grieves.

But those who give their all in trust
are raised from dust.

Irene Zimmerman

DEATH AND RESURRECTION

A broken tree, strewn across a stream . . .
I was not witness to the ancient pain
that brought it down
(the lightning, tortured rain),
but sense a kinship here, recall a dream
I once was caught in—twisted undergrowth,
frenzied insects, slimy clutching clay;
of being brought through that to Calvary
and finding Jesus hanging on His cross!

The broken tree is overgrown with moss.
The agony has greened to ecstasy.

CONTEMPLATION

The longest journey of all
covers the shortest ground:
the way is to sit still
and let oneself be found.

IN YOUR WOMB, MOTHER-GOD

This promise-of-me
growing in the dark,
swimming in the fluid of
Geborgenheit,
cannot see Your Face as yet,
but curls to sleep
in perfect confidence.

FLUTE NOTE

When I was a child, my mother told
of a dream she'd had when she lived
in an Augsburg tenement house:
      one of her daughters
      went to the woods
      to play her flute.
      A clear note winged
      through the trees
      and flew across the sea.

Walking our Iowa woods
on Sunday afternoons, flute in hand,
I heard and played that note.

Now the dream has grown:
      I *am* the note
      playing the hollow reed,
      readying
      till the One who breathed me
      (is breathing me still)
      will give me wings to fly Home:

      one long whole note blown clear.

FLOWERING FIELDS

I used to keep You sweetly shut away
(serenely silent, secret, safely graved)
behind a well-locked tabernacle door.
There I would come to light my candles, pour
my tears and well-versed words out, and feel saved.

That worn path I plodded day by day
(heading for a lonely golden gate)
imprisoned me from free and sunlit air,
from flowering fields where
You are alive illimitably and wait.

BE-COMING

Morning by morning,
year by year,
I edge near the rim
of myself and peer
into the dark from where
my life springs up,
knowing, more and more,
moment by moment,
my hollow core
and growing aware
of You be-coming me there.

Someday I may hear
an encouraging "Ready?
Let go—I'll catch you!"
or perhaps arms will steady
my childish fear
and carry me through,
leaving behind
that outer rim
for others to find
and bury.

SEASHELL MATINS

Infinitely new, all-loving God,
who will You say this morning that You are?
I look out from my little sheltered world
and hope to catch a glimpse of You, to tell
the other blind what this small *I* can see.

You pass by!
Save, O God, this particle of part.
Your Presence inarticulates my mind,
inundates my shallow shell of heart.

"YAHWEH, MY HERITAGE, MY CUP"
(Ps 16)

After the first snow of this decembered
time, the textured grass is spread
like Irish linen on the field You
set before me. I feast on trees
moving in wind and wander down
to drink the wine stored in
dark root cellars.
Your Spirit
warms
my
blood
O
God!
O God!

FLUTE PLAYER

On such a quiet day I fleeting feel
Your ever-Presence stirring in my roots,
rising, flowing through my branches,
and I become a thousand singing flutes!

GOD, YOU HAVE SO MANY WAYS

God, You have so many ways
to make Your presence known:
a pebble in the hand,
the way the wind has blown
across a field,
ridges in the sand. . . .

If I were caught by hurricanes
and whirled to near despair,
I'll bet You'd find some burning bush
to tell me You were there.

BURNING BUSH

As little girl I learned, my God, that You
sat in a judgment seat from which You swayed
Your scepter. You were absolute.
No one escaped Your justice. To dispute
this truth was heresy—"Woe be
to you," etc. They taught me well.
Each night I knelt beside my bed and prayed
I would not die in sin and burn in hell.

Perhaps they told me, but I failed to learn
Yours is another kind of fire: a shout
across the desert miles, a burn
of love that never never will die out.

LEGACY

My old uncle gave a rose to me.
I almost cried,
knowing he couldn't see
the brown-stained petals on the underside.

At ninety years he dug the flowerbed—
"My legacy for other people's eyes,"
he said. "I'll be dead
before the bushes come to any size."

Now they've grown green and full,
and he at ninety-five
still works the soil,
still wonderfully alive.

All his life he gardened—beauty grows
wherever he has been.
I hold the full-blown rose
in my heart and pen

and know that when he's gone
the fragrance of his life will linger on.

HOMECOMING

As I was walking home alone last night
a breath of lilac caught me by surprise
and flew me back with Peter Pan delight
to front lawn evenings of my childhood years.

Seduction came to question: If you could
unlive the years you've groaned through,
            would you choose
to be a child again (the lilac fragrance
tempting me to grasp that innocence)?

I finally saw my life: a mystery of
a wandering sheep forever loved and found,
and rather than that lilac paradise,
chose instead this firm forgiving ground.

THANKSGIVING AT YEAR'S END

The year is finished now. I bring it home—
a fragrant winter apple—taut, red-skinned,
firm, filled with sun and rain and wind—
and hold it for this while, remembering. . . .

In spring it was a small embudded dream.
It wore pink-petaled swaddling in May.
By June, not pretty anymore, its virtue lay
in clinging to the tree through every weather
and curious bird (come perilously close)
and drinking in the sweet or bitter juice
given it day by day.
Finally in fall, still blushing from
late summer's tender touch when
                              cold winds caught it,
let it know full blast
that life is not all ecstasy and love,
it reached maturity.

I've brought it home and slowly—savoring
the sweet white pulp, the seed, the peel—
eat gratefully this fully ripened meal.